LANGUAGE!®

The Comprehensive Literacy Curriculum

D1506862

Assessment:
Content Mastery

Book D

Jane Fell Greene, Ed.D.

SOPRIS WEST EDUCATIONAL SERVICES
A CAMBIUM LEARNING COMPANY

BOSTON, MA • NEW YORK, NY • LONGMONT, CO

08 07 06 05   10 9 8 7 6 5 4 3 2

Editorial Director: Nancy Chapel Eberhardt
Word and Phrase Selection: Judy Fell Woods
English Learners: Jennifer Wells Greene
Lesson Development: Sheryl Ferlito, Donna Lutz, Isabel Wesley
Text Selection: Sara Buckerfield, Jim Cloonan

ISBN 1-59318-297-X Book D

Printed in the United States of America

Published and distributed by

SOPRIS
WEST
EDUCATIONAL SERVICES

4093 Specialty Place • Longmont, CO 80504 • (303) 651-2829
www.sopriswest.com

Table of Contents

Name _____

Vowel Digraphs

Total Number
Correct _____ /10

Lesson 5 • Step 1

Listen to each word your teacher says. Repeat the word. Write the **vowel digraph** for the long vowel sound you hear in each word.

1. _____   6. _____

2. _____   7. _____

3. _____   8. _____

4. _____   9. _____

5. _____   10. _____

Name _____

Spelling Posttest 1

Number
Correct _____ /15

Lesson 5 • Step 2

Write the words your teacher says.

1. _____   9. _____

2. _____   10. _____

3. _____   11. _____

4. _____   12. _____

5. _____   13. _____

6. _____   14. _____

7. _____   15. _____

8. _____

Name _____

Homophones

Lesson 9 • Step 3

Read the homophones in the **Word Bank**.

Word Bank				
rode	waste	tale	male	pale
road	waist	tail	mail	pail

Read each sentence and select a word from the **Word Bank** that makes sense in the blank. Fill in the blank with a homophone from the **Word Bank**.

1. We _____ our bikes down the dirt _____ .

2. The young _____ drove the _____ truck.

3. Don't _____ the supplies. Put the extra in the _____ .

4. My friend looked _____ just before he tied his coat around his _____ .

5. Her sister told a _____ about how the dog's _____ got hurt.

Prefixes and Suffixes

Lesson 9 • Step 3

Do the example with your teacher. Read each word pair. Think about the meaning of the prefix or suffix in both words. Fill in the bubble that matches the meaning of the affix.

> **Example:** teacher: trainer
> What does the suffix in this word pair mean?
> ○ A. something that
> ○ B. someone who
> ○ C. more

Fill in Answer B for **someone who.** The suffix -er means "**someone who.**" Finish the remaining items independently.

1. **entertainment: shipment**
   ○ A. the act of
   ○ B. the condition of
   ○ C. someone who

2. **deeper : greener**
   ○ A. most
   ○ B. something that
   ○ C. more

3. **finalist: medalist**
   ○ A. something that
   ○ B. someone who
   ○ C. greater than normal

4. **thickness: dampness**
   ○ A. the condition of
   ○ B. something that
   ○ C. the act of

5. **painless: sleepless**
   ○ A. opposite
   ○ B. to become
   ○ C. without

6. **deepen: darken**
   ○ A. opposite
   ○ B. full of
   ○ C. to become

7. **midyear: midterm**
   ○ A. middle
   ○ B. in front of
   ○ C. above

8. **forecast: foresee**
   ○ A. above
   ○ B. before
   ○ C. middle

9. **misprint: miscalculate**
   ○ A. before
   ○ B. wrong
   ○ C. too much

10. **oversleep: overdue**
    ○ A. beyond
    ○ B. wrong
    ○ C. before

Name _____

Noun and Adjective Suffixes

Lesson 9 • Step 4

Two points per item.

Read each sentence and identify the word with a suffix. Underline the base word and circle the suffix. Decide if the suffix makes the word into a noun or an adjective. Copy the suffix into the correct column.

	Noun	Adjective
1. The hopeful athlete put on her uniform.	_____	_____
2. There was an odd quietness in the stadium.	_____	_____
3. The runner found this pre-race time difficult.	_____	_____
4. The girl did not want to make a careless mistake.	_____	_____
5. She did want to be the gold medalist.	_____	_____

Predicate Nominative

Read each sentence. Decide if the underlined noun is used as a direct object or a predicate nominative. Put an X in the correct column.

	Direct Object	Predicate Nominative
6. Women's track was a new <u>event</u>.	_____	_____
7. Betty Robinson was a high school <u>athlete</u>.	_____	_____
8. She had a devoted <u>trainer</u>.	_____	_____
9. Betty was the 100-meter <u>champion</u>.	_____	_____
10. She won the gold <u>medal</u>.	_____	_____
11. Squeaky was also a <u>champion</u>.	_____	_____
12. She ran <u>races</u> at the playground.	_____	_____
13. Squeaky is Raymond's <u>babysitter</u>.	_____	_____
14. Raymond and Squeaky are <u>siblings</u>.	_____	_____
15. They spend <u>time</u> together.	_____	_____

Name _____

Spelling Posttest 2

Total Number
Correct _____ /15

Lesson 10 • Step 2

Write the sentences your teacher says.

1. _____

2. _____

3. _____

4. _____

5. _____

Unit 20

Name _____

Vowel Digraphs

Lesson 5 • Step 1

Listen to each word your teacher says. Repeat the word. Write the **vowel digraph** for the long vowel sound you hear in each word.

1. _____

2. _____

3. _____

4. _____

5. _____

6. _____

7. _____

8. _____

9. _____

10. _____

Name _____

Spelling Posttest 1

Total Number
Correct _____ /15

Lesson 5 • Step 2

Write the words your teacher says.

1. _____

2. _____

3. _____

4. _____

5. _____

6. _____

7. _____

8. _____

9. _____

10. _____

11. _____

12. _____

13. _____

14. _____

15. _____

Name _____

Homophones

Lesson 9 • Step 3

Read the homophones in the **Word Bank**.

Word Bank				
brake	grate	meet	reed	week
break	great	meat	read	weak

Read each sentence and select a word from the **Word Bank** that makes sense in the blank.
Fill in the blank with a homophone from the **Word Bank**.

1. Please _____ the cheese for our pizza.

2. Be careful so that you don't _____ the china.

3. You did a _____ job on your history test!

4. Did you _____ the substitute teacher?

5. The _____ vibrates when air is blown against it.

6. Mysteries are my favorite books to _____ .

7. The video will be released next _____ .

8. Fish is not usually included in the _____ group.

9. It is important to _____ at all railroad crossings.

10. I am too _____ to lift that by myself.

Morphology

Lesson 9 • Step 3

Read the words in the **Word Bank**. Note the different suffixes on the same root.

Word Bank				
export	exporting	forming	retract	deform
detract	detracted	extract	reporter	reform

Read each sentence. Choose a word from the **Word Bank** to replace the underlined phrase. Write the word on the line. Check your answer by reading the sentence with the word you chose in place.

1. Many American companies <u>send</u> their goods <u>to other countries</u>. _____

2. The dentist will have to <u>pull out</u> my tooth. _____

3. To tell lies about someone will <u>take away</u> from that person's good name. _____

4. The acid rain will <u>ruin the shape</u> of the trees' leaves. _____

5. My cousins are <u>making the shape of</u> a sand castle. _____

6. The man was in charge of <u>sending</u> goods <u>out</u> of the country for sale. _____

7. You must <u>pull back</u> that statement because it is wrong. _____

8. The constant chatter while the band played <u>took away</u> from our enjoyment. _____

9. The <u>person who carried news back</u> was late for the deadline. _____

10. The judge wanted the city to <u>change the form of</u> its jury selection process. _____

Name _____

Irregular Verbs

Number
Correct _____ /10

Two points per item.

Lesson 9 • Step 4

Read each sentence. Underline the past tense verb. Write the past, present, and future forms of the verb in the chart below.

1. He paid for his ticket to the play.

2. The older woman spoke about her early life.

3. The family ate a simple meal together.

4. The boys left for the soccer game.

5. Lorraine Hansberry grew up in Chicago.

Yesterday	Today	Tomorrow
Past	Present	Future

Irregular Past Tense	Present Tense	Future Tense

Predicate Nominative and Predicate Adjective

Number Correct _____ /5

Lesson 9 • Step 4

Read each sentence. Decide if the underlined word is a predicate nominative or a predicate adjective. Put an X in the correct box.

	Sentence	Predicate Nominative	Predicate Adjective
6.	Lorraine Hansberry was a <u>playwright</u>.		
7.	She was very <u>successful</u>.		
8.	She is <u>famous</u> today.		
9.	She was a gifted <u>writer</u>.		
10.	She was very <u>young</u> when she wrote "A Raisin in the Sun."		

Commas in Series, Dates, and Addresses

Number Correct _____ /5

Read each sentence. Fill in the blanks for the last two sentences.
Place commas where needed.

11. Lorraine Hansberry was a young talented and successful writer.

12. On April 12 1861 the Civil War started.

13. It ended on April 9 1865.

14. My date of birth is _____

15. My home address is _____

_____

Total Number Correct _____ /20

Spelling Posttest 2

Total Number
Correct _____ /15

Lesson 10 • Step 2

Write the sentences your teacher says.

1. _____

2. _____

3. _____

4. _____

_____

5. _____

_____

Schwa

Lesson 5 • Step 1

Read each word aloud. Underline the stressed syllable in each word. Circle any vowel or vowels reduced to **schwa** in each word. Circle the letter for the sentence that explains the **schwa** condition.

1. **aside**
   a. **Schwa** is in the unstressed syllable of a two-syllable word.
   b. The letter **a** at the beginning or end of a word is often reduced to **schwa**.
   c. Neither

2. **subscribe**
   a. **Schwa** is in the unstressed syllable of a two-syllable word.
   b. The letter **a** at the beginning or end of a word is often reduced to **schwa**.
   c. Neither

3. **correct**
   a. **Schwa** is in the unstressed syllable of a two-syllable word.
   b. The letter **a** at the beginning or end of a word is often reduced to **schwa**.
   c. Neither

4. **arena**
   a. **Schwa** is in the unstressed syllable of a two-syllable word.
   b. The letter **a** at the beginning or end of a word is often reduced to **schwa**.
   c. Neither

5. **form**
   a. **Schwa** is in the unstressed syllable of a two-syllable word.
   b. The letter **a** at the beginning or end of a word is often reduced to **schwa**.
   c. Neither

6. **canal**
   a. **Schwa** is in the unstressed syllable of a two-syllable word.
   b. The letter **a** at the beginning or end of a word is often reduced to **schwa**.
   c. Neither

7. **quota**
   a. **Schwa** is in the unstressed syllable of a two-syllable word.
   b. The letter **a** at the beginning or end of a word is often reduced to **schwa**.
   c. Neither

Schwa (continued)

Lesson 5 • Step 1

8. **part**
   a. **Schwa** is in the unstressed syllable of a two-syllable word.
   b. The letter **a** at the beginning or end of a word is often reduced to **schwa**.
   c. Neither

9. **apart**
   a. **Schwa** is in the unstressed syllable of a two-syllable word.
   b. The letter **a** at the beginning or end of a word is often reduced to **schwa**.
   c. Neither

10. **subtract**
    a. **Schwa** is in the unstressed syllable of a two-syllable word.
    b. The letter **a** at the beginning or end of a word is often reduced to **schwa**.
    c. Neither

Spelling Posttest 1

Lesson 5 • Step 2

Write the words your teacher says.

1. _____

2. _____

3. _____

4. _____

5. _____

6. _____

7. _____

8. _____

9. _____

10. _____

11. _____

12. _____

13. _____

14. _____

15. _____

Name _____

Antonyms

Lesson 9 • Step 3

Read the words in the **Word Bank**.

Word Bank				
active	violent	inactive	substitute	identical
permanent	incomplete	different	done	dependent
seldom	separate	difficult	antonym	recommend

Complete each word pair by writing an antonym from the **Word Bank** on the line.

1. busy: _____

2. finished: _____

3. disapprove: _____

4. often: _____

5. temporary: _____

6. calm: _____

7. similar: _____

8. opposite: _____

9. independent: _____

10. uncomplicated: _____

Morphology

Lesson 9 • Step 3

Read the words in the **Word Bank**. Note the different suffixes on the same root.

Word Bank				
conducting	induct	scripting	prescribing	inscribing
conductor	inducted	scripted	prescribes	inscribed

Read each sentence. Choose a word from the **Word Bank** to replace the underlined phrase. Write the word on the line. Check your answer by reading the sentence with the word you chose in place.

1. The students got together and <u>wrote down</u> their own play. _____

2. The sculptor built the monument and <u>wrote in</u> names on it. _____

3. The band members liked the <u>person who was leading them</u>. _____

4. Some groups <u>lead in</u> new members into their groups with special ceremonies. _____

5. The doctor <u>writes down</u> the medicine the parents must give the baby. _____

6. The school committee was <u>doing</u> business in the town. _____

7. The instructor was <u>writing down</u> a plan for us to follow. _____

8. The new member was given a club sweatshirt after she had been <u>led in</u>. _____

9. We are <u>writing down</u> possible things to say to our teacher. _____

10. It is against school rules to be <u>writing in</u> our names on the desks. _____

Name _____

Nouns and Adjectives

Lesson 9 • Step 4

Read each sentence. Decide whether each underlined word is a noun or an adjective.
Copy the underlined word into the correct column.

1. For three <u>years</u>, Anne Frank's family lived in an <u>annex</u>.

2. Their life was <u>stressful</u> and <u>harsh</u>.

3. Anne wrote in her <u>diary</u> of their <u>grim</u> state.

4. She saw her <u>father</u> as her <u>protector</u>.

5. Anne was a <u>careful</u> and <u>observant</u> teenager.

Noun	Adjective

Predicate Nominative and Predicate Adjective

Number Correct _____ /5

Lesson 9 • Step 4

Read each sentence. Decide if the underlined word is a predicate nominative or a predicate adjective. Write **PN** for predicate nominative or **PA** for predicate adjective above the word.

1. His brother was <u>older</u>.

2. The angry father was <u>scary</u>.

3. His mother was his favorite <u>parent</u>.

4. The boys were <u>brothers</u>.

5. The brother's trick was <u>mean</u>.

Commas in Series

Number Correct _____ /5

Lesson 9 • Step 4

Read each sentence. Underline each word group in the series. Place commas where needed.

1. Anne Frank's diary tells of her family her feelings and her hopes.

2. She observed her sister and brother wrote of their relationships and dreamed about their futures.

3. Before the war, Anne lived in Frankfurt had a comfortable life and had a secure childhood.

4. If you read Anne's diary, take time to note her careful observations her conflicted feelings about her mother and her growth over time.

5. Today, when people read **"The Diary of a Young Girl,"** they usually are moved by her youth by her sensitivity and by her clearly expressed feelings.

Total Number Correct _____ /20

Name _____

Spelling Posttest 2

Lesson 10 • Step 2

Write the sentences your teacher says.

1. _____

2. _____

   _____

3. _____

   _____

4. _____

5. _____

Name _____

Answering Questions

Lesson 10 • Step 5

A Family Coat of Arms

Coats of arms were created long ago. They were made during the times of knights. In the twelfth century, European soldiers put on armor when they prepared for battle. The armor kept them from being easily hurt by the enemy. But this armor also made it quite difficult for soldiers to recognize each other. The armor covered a soldier's face and head. Soldiers began wearing a "coat of arms." A coat of arms was a piece of clothing. It was worn over the armor. It was like a shirt or a coat. Symbols were marked on this coat. The symbols helped to identify the knight who was wearing it. This is similar to the way that numbers printed on jerseys help to identify football players.

The coat of arms had many parts. The shield was the heart of the coat of arms. Within the shield were symbols that represented a family. Colors also represented a family. Above the shield was the crest. The crest was a symbol or animal that served as a family mascot. The motto completed the coat of arms. This sentence expressed a family's ideal or goal. It was written on a banner. The banner crossed the bottom of the shield. These symbols were passed along from generation to generation.

1. Assess the need for wearing a coat of arms during battle.

   _____

   _____

   _____

2. Today, some families display their family coat of arms on a wall in their home. One part of a coat of arms is the motto. Tell what your motto would be if your family had a coat of arms. Explain the meaning of your motto.

   _____

   _____

Anwering Questions

Lesson 10 • Step 5

Diamonds in Technology

Diamonds are being made in laboratories. They are not being made by natural forces. They are being made by humans. Most of these diamonds will never wind up as jewelry. They are being made for use in technology.

What makes diamond so special? First, it is very hard. It is the hardest known substance. It can scratch anything. Nothing else can scratch it. Diamond conducts heat. It conducts sound. It conducts both better than any other material. Music sounds better when heard through high-tech speakers with diamond membranes. In addition, diamond doesn't conduct electricity well. This means it can be used as an insulator. It is also clear. A person can see through it. It can be used as a strong coating. Finally, diamond won't break down when mixed with any known chemical.

Scientists have been using diamond's special qualities. Someday soon, you may wear sunglasses coated with diamond. You might find yourself looking into a computer screen coated with diamond. This screen might be attached to a computer. The computer's memory might be stored on diamond instead of silicon. The sunglasses will be scratchproof. The screen will be brighter. The computer will be more powerful.

---

3. Justify the use of diamonds in technology. Include at least two examples to support your answer. Be sure to cite evidence from the text.

   _____

   _____

4. Glass is used in many products today. Compare the qualities of diamonds versus glass.

   _____

   _____

5. Sunglasses coated with diamond are products that would last longer. Predict at least three other products that would last longer if made with diamond.

   _____

   _____

Final Consonant + _le_ and Vowel Digraphs

Lesson 5 • Step 1

Write the **final consonant** + _le_ syllable in each word your teacher says.

1. _____

2. _____

3. _____

4. _____

5. _____

Write the **vowel digraph** for the vowel sound you hear in each word your teacher says.

6. _____

7. _____

8. _____

9. _____

10. _____

Name _____

Spelling Posttest 1

Total Number
Correct _____ /15

Lesson 5 • Step 2

Write the words your teacher says.

1. _____   9. _____

2. _____   10. _____

3. _____   11. _____

4. _____   12. _____

5. _____   13. _____

6. _____   14. _____

7. _____   15. _____

8. _____

Name _____

Attributes

Lesson 9 • Step 3

Two points per item.

Choose a word that completes the attribute pair. Write your answer in the blank.

1. eagle: _____ **as** _____ **:fur**

    ○ a. beagle   ○ b. threaten   ○ c. wings   ○ d. bark

2. table: _____ **as cabinet:** _____

    ○ a. label   ○ b. legs   ○ c. tangle   ○ d. handle

3. grapes: _____ **as** _____ **:red**

    ○ a. purple   ○ b. apple   ○ c. bread   ○ d. wagon

4. breakfast: _____ **as dinner:** _____

    ○ a. evening   ○ b. toast   ○ c. morning   ○ d. table

5. airplane: _____ **as bicycle:** _____

    ○ a. pedal   ○ b. propeller   ○ c. train   ○ d. car

Name _____

Word Meanings

Total Number	
Correct _____ /10	

Lesson 9 • Step 3

Read the meanings of the word parts in the box. Read the list of words and the list of definitions. Write the letter for the correct definition in the blank.

pro = look forward	able = to say, tell	spect = to see, look	dis = not, absence, remove
dict = to say, tell	pre = before	ous = characterized by	tract = to pull

Word

1. prospect _____

2. predictable _____

3. vigorous _____

4. disorder _____

5. humorous _____

6. disrespectable _____

7. protract _____

8. discharge _____

9. famous _____

10. distract _____

Definition

a. remove the pull, lose focus

b. absence of order

c. able to tell beforehand

d. something expected, looked forward to

e. to remove the charge

f. not able to respect

g. characterized by fame

h. pull forward, lengthen

i. characterized by vigor

j. characterized by humor

Phrasal Verbs

Number Correct _____ /10

Lesson 9 • Step 4

Two points per item.

Read each sentence. Underline the phrasal verb. Copy it in the first column. Write its meaning in the second column.

	Phrasal Verb	Definition
1. I ran into an old school friend.	_____	_____
2. We puzzled over the clues in the mystery.	_____	_____
3. Please fill out the form accurately.	_____	_____
4. You can pick out your favorite food.	_____	_____
5. My brother made up an excuse when he was late.	_____	_____

Predicate Nominative, Predicate Adjective, and Direct Object

Number Correct _____ /5

Lesson 9 • Step 4

Read each sentence. Decide whether the underlined word is a predicate nominative, a predicate adjective, or a direct object. Put an X in the correct column.

	Predicate Nominative	Predicate Adjective	Direct Object
6. The boy was <u>curious</u> about the crime.	_____	_____	_____
7. The police caught <u>Stockton</u> in the building.	_____	_____	_____
8. Larry's father was an <u>inspector</u>.	_____	_____	_____
9. Larry was <u>nervous</u> when the police arrived.	_____	_____	_____
10. The thief stole <u>jewels</u> from the store.	_____	_____	_____

Name _____

Commas in Series, Dates, and Addresses

Lesson 9 • Step 4

Read each sentence. Place commas where needed.

11. The building was completed on Saturday July 3 1993.

12. Our school's address is 25 Lincoln Road Concord PA 22222.

13. My sister disguised herself came to the party alone and surprised everyone.

14. We study biology math chemistry English and history.

15. Wednesday June 11 2006 was the last day of their project.

**Total Number
Correct _____ /20**

Name _____

Spelling Posttest 2

Lesson 10 • Step 2

Write the sentences your teacher says.

1. _____

2. _____

_____

3. _____

_____

4. _____

_____

5. _____

Name _____

Diphthong Syllables

Number Correct _____ /10

Lesson 5 • Step 1

Listen to each word your teacher says. Repeat the word. Identify the position of the / *oi* / or / *ou* / sound in each word. Write each word in the column for its spelling pattern: **oi**, **oy**, **ou**, or **ow**.

oi	oy	ou	ow

Name _____

Spelling Posttest 1

Lesson 5 • Step 2

Write the words your teacher says.

1. _____

2. _____

3. _____

4. _____

5. _____

6. _____

7. _____

8. _____

9. _____

10. _____

11. _____

12. _____

13. _____

14. _____

15. _____

Name _____

Synonyms

Lesson 9 • Step 3

Read the words in the **Word Bank**.

Word Bank				
crowd	operate	poison	powerful	sweet
transport	sour	power	awake	couch
spoil	powerless	reject	drowsy	allow

Complete each word pair by writing a synonym from the **Word Bank** on the line.

1. toxic: _____

2. bitter: _____

3. sleepy: _____

4. sofa: _____

5. weak: _____

6. strong: _____

7. decline: _____

8. tolerate: _____

9. move: _____

10. run: _____

Word Meanings

Lesson 9 • Step 3

Read each sentence. Circle the meaning of the underlined word.

1. If **external** means "outside," what does **internal** mean?

   a. exterior   b. inside   c. over

2. If **exhale** means "to breathe out," what does **inhale** mean?

   a. sniff   b. breathless   c. breathe in

3. If **verbal** means "about words," what does **nonverbal** mean?

   a. without words   b. wordy   c. verb

4. If **stick** means "to attach," what does **unstick** mean?

   a. glue   b. detach   c. sticky

5. If **press** means "to squeeze," what does **express** mean?

   a. squeeze out   b. train   c. juice

6. If the root **mit** means "to send," what does **emit** mean?

   a. receive   b. gone   c. send out

7. If **satisfactory** means "all right," what does **unsatisfactory** mean?

   a. satisfied   b. bad   c. good

8. If **similar** means "alike," what does **dissimilar** mean?

   a. same   b. different   c. copy

9. If the root **vade** means "to go," what does **pervade** mean?

   a. go through   b. permit   c. go in

10. If the root **gress** means "a step," what does **progress** mean?

    a. stairs   b. a step forward   c. a step backward

Prepositions and Objects of Prepositions

Number Correct _____ /10

Lesson 9 • Step 4

Two points per item.

Read each sentence. Underline the preposition in the sentence.
Circle the object of the preposition.

1. The ball stayed within the boundaries.

2. The car races toward the empty parking spot.

3. Kenneth got flattened beneath Bill Patchet.

4. Everyone but Kenneth played football.

5. The stolen car was found minus its wheels.

Compound Predicate Nominative and Adjective, and Compound Direct Object

Number Correct _____ /5

Lesson 9, Step 4

Read each sentence. Decide if the underlined section is a compound predicate nominative, a compound predicate adjective, or a compound direct object. Put an X in the correct column.

	Compound Predicate Nominative	Compound Predicate Adjective	Compound Direct Object
6. Kenneth was <u>thoughtful and kind</u>.	_____	_____	_____
7. Ramdas followed <u>Gandhi and satyagraha</u>.	_____	_____	_____
8. Satyagraha is <u>peaceful and nonviolent</u>.	_____	_____	_____
9. Bill Patchet was <u>a football player and a bully</u>.	_____	_____	_____
10. Sarah drove <u>Kenneth and Ramdas</u> to the school.	_____	_____	_____

Name _____

Phrasal Verbs

Lesson 9 • Step 4

Read each sentence. Underline the phrasal verb. Circle its correct meaning.

11. The writer threw her first draft away.

   a. file   b. rewrite   c. discard

12. When I made the salad dressing, I left an important spice out.

   a. omitted   b. included   c. trashed

13. The man turned the offer down on his house.

   a. took   b. rejected   c. trusted

14. The students set the display up quickly and carefully.

   a. removed   b. arranged   c. expanded

15. The fireworks blew up with an enormous bang.

   a. destroyed   b. fizzled   c. exploded

Name _____

Spelling Posttest 2

Lesson 10 • Step 2

Write the sentences your teacher says.

1. _____

_____

2. _____

_____

3. _____

4. _____

5. _____

_____

Spelling Posttest 1

Number Correct _____ /15

Lesson 5 • Step 2

Write the words your teacher says.

1. _____
2. _____
3. _____
4. _____
5. _____
6. _____
7. _____
8. _____

9. _____
10. _____
11. _____
12. _____
13. _____
14. _____
15. _____

Spelling Posttest 2

Number Correct _____ /15

Lesson 10 • Step 2

Write the sentences your teacher says.

1. _____
2. _____
3. _____
4. _____
   _____
5. _____